100 QUESTIONS about DOGS

and all the answers too!

Written and Illustrated by
Simon Abbott

PETER PAUPER PRESS, INC.
White Plains, New York

For Dash, The top dog of the street

PETER PAUPER PRESS

In 1928, at the age of twenty-two, Peter Beilenson began printing books on a small press in the basement of his parents' home in Larchmont, New York. Peter—and later, his wife, Edna—sought to create fine books that sold at "prices even a pauper could afford."

Today, still family owned and operated, Peter Pauper Press continues to honor our founders' legacy of quality, value, and fun for big kids and small kids alike.

Library of Congress Cataloging-in-Publication Data

Names: Abbott, Simon, 1967- author, illustrator.
Title: 100 questions about dogs : and all the answers too! / written and illustrated by Simon Abbott.
Other titles: One hundred questions about dogs
Description: White Plains, New York : Peter Pauper Press, Inc., [2021] | Series: 100 questions | Audience: Ages 7 | Audience: Grades 2-3 | Summary: "What does it mean when a dog barks? How did dogs first become our best friends? Why is a dog's nose always wet? You can find fascinating facts about our canine companions, including the answers to these questions and over 100 more, in this question-and-answer adventure! Learn what makes your pawsome partners tick, pick up tips and tricks on how to care for your furry best friend, and more! Along the way, you'll discover doggy jokes and incredible tails . . . I mean, tails!"-- Provided by publisher.
Identifiers: LCCN 2020038355 | ISBN 9781441335371 (hardcover)
Subjects: LCSH: Dogs--Juvenile literature.
Classification: LCC SF426.5 .A23 2021 | DDC 636.7--dc23
LC record available at https://lccn.loc.gov/2020038355

Designed by Heather Zschock

Text and illustrations copyright © 2021 by Simon Abbott

Published by Peter Pauper Press, Inc.
202 Mamaroneck Avenue
White Plains, New York 10601 USA

Published in the United Kingdom and Europe by Peter Pauper Press, Inc.
c/o White Pebble International
Unit 2, Plot 11 Terminus Rd.
Chichester, West Sussex PO19 8TX, UK

ISBN 978-1-4413-3537-1
Manufactured for Peter Pauper Press, Inc.
Printed in China

7 6 5 4 3 2 1

Visit us at www.peterpauper.com

WELCOME TO THE WONDERFUL WORLD OF DOGS!

Let's get the low-down on these
super-sniffers and terrific tail-waggers!

Why is a dog's nose wet?

Which dog has the longest and lick-iest tongue?

How tall is the world's tallest dog?

Which brave breeds make fur-midable lifeguards?

It's time to turn the page and brush up
on some doggy data.

Let's go!

FROM HEAD TO TAIL

Let's begin with an ear to paw check-up! How do dogs function?

How useful are those big, floppy ears of theirs?

A dog's hearing is around four times greater than that of a human! Dogs can hone in on tiny sounds from great distances, and can hear a wide range of frequencies. The muscles in a dog's ear allow it to turn, lift, and lower each ear independently. That's why if you make a stimulating sound (like opening a can of dog food), a hungry hound will react in 0.06 of a second!

OLFACTORY BULB

BRAIN

OLFACTORY NERVE

NOSTRILS

NERVE CELLS

What about a dog's sense of smell?

A dog's nose is incredible! It's thought that a dog's sense of smell can be as much as 100,000 times better than a human's, thanks to noses packed with more nerves and scent receptors (tiny cells that pick up smells). Each doggy nostril can smell separate things. Dog noses can even detect temperature!

Why is a dog's nose always wet?

 A dog's nose secretes a sticky mucus, which picks up tiny scent particles from whatever it's sniffing.

 A dog licks its nose to keep it moist, which helps it pick up scents better. Washing its nose gives a dog a second "whiff" of the smells inside its mouth, too. Dogs also lick their noses accidentally when they're eating.

3. Dogs love to explore, so on a walk they may have their snout in a puddle or on wet grass.

4. A dog's nose is a cooling system. If it gets hot, it will sweat through its nose.

Do dogs have exceptional eyesight?

For a dog, vision is not as important as hearing and smell. What a human could see from 75 feet (23 m) away, a dog could only see from 20 feet (6 m) away. Dogs see fewer colors than humans, but they have better night vision and can see a bigger area at once.

CANINE   MOLARS

PREMOLARS

INCISORS

How many teeth does a dog have?

A grown dog has 42 teeth, compared to 32 in an adult human. There are four types:

INCISORS — Used for grooming, and for pulling meat from a bone.

CANINES — Four pointy, "fang-like" teeth. These are great for puncturing and holding on to things.

PREMOLARS — A dog uses these for chewing and shearing.

MOLARS — These flat teeth at the back of the mouth are used for grinding and chopping.

How strong is a dog's jaw?

It depends on the breed. A Rottweiler tops the leader board with 328 pounds of bite pressure per inch (or **psi**). The average human chomps down with a force of 162 psi, while the nippy Nile crocodile snaps its mouth shut at a powerful 5,000 psi. Keep away from the River Nile!

FRONT PAW · BACK PAW · DIGITAL PADS · METACARPAL PAD · METATARSAL PAD · CARPAL PAD

What are the pads on a dog's paw for?

Protection! The pads work as shock absorbers to cushion the bones and joints in the foot. The **carpal pad** is a "brake" to help a dog slow down over slippery or steep surfaces. The pads have a layer of fatty tissue to insulate the foot against extreme temperatures, and sweat glands help the dog cool off. Paw-fect!

How many bones does a dog have?
Humans have 206 bones. Do you think a dog has more, or fewer? It's more!
A canine has around 319 bones, with as many as 23 in its tail alone.

Why are some dogs bigger, stronger, or faster than others?
It's breeding. Just as people may look different depending
on their parents, dogs differ depending on what their parents
were like. Different dog **breeds**, or types, have different traits.
Muscular Greyhounds can sprint up to 45 mph (72 km/h), while
a leisurely Pug lags behind at 5–10 mph (8–16 km/h).

CANINE COMMUNICATION

Can we translate a dog's growls, barks, and whimpers? What is a dog trying to tell us with every tail wag? Let's find out!

How can we tell if a dog is happy?

A dog uses its tail to communicate. When a dog is relaxed, its tail will be in its "neutral'" position, which differs between breeds. If a dog is nervous, it will hold its tail lower than its normal position, and will tuck it under its body if scared. A tail held straight out means that the dog is interested in something, such as a rabbit!

What does a wagging tail mean?

Excitement! As the dog gets even more excited, the tail wags faster and faster. Research has found that when dogs communicate with other dogs, a tail swinging to the right expresses good feelings, and a tail leaning to the left means a bad mood.

What does a relaxed, happy dog look like?

1. **Relaxed body posture** · Smooth hair · Open mouth · Ears in a natural position · Normal-shaped eyes · Wagging tail

2. **Dog wants to play** · Bottom raised · May bark excitedly · Ears in natural position · Normal shaped eyes · High, wagging tail

3. **Dog standing evenly on all four paws** · Smooth hair · Attentive and alert face · Relaxed open mouth · Wagging tail

What does a worried dog look like?

1. **Body and head low** · Ears back · Dog yawning · Tail tucked under

2. **Dog lying down** · Avoids eye contact · Ears back · Licks lips

3. **Sits with head lowered** · Ears back · No eye contact · Yawning · Raises front paw · Tail tucked away

What does an angry and upset dog look like?

1. **Weight forward with a tense body posture** · Hair raised · Staring eyes, with big dark pupils · Ears up · Wrinkled nose · Tail up and stiff

2. **Dog crouching down** · Ears flat · Teeth showing · Tail between its legs

3. **Dog standing with weight on back feet** · Head tilted upward · Mouth tense · Teeth exposed with lips back · Snarling · Staring eyes · Ears back and down

Some dogs can voice their feelings. What do different dog barks mean?
Dogs bark, whine, and growl when they are excited, frightened,
lonely, surprised, irritated, or trying to grab your attention.
They have different barks for different moods.

What does a low-pitched bark mean?
The dog is serious! It might be warning off intruders or frightened by a stranger.
A higher-pitched bark is more excited and playful. A lonely dog also makes a
high-pitched bark, which can develop into a sad yelp.

What if a dog is barking over and over?
It depends on the length of the pause between each bark or growl.
Constant, rapid barking might mean there's a big problem, or a dispute
over territory. If there are long pauses between each woof, then the
dog is feeling lonesome and wants some company.

Not all dogs communicate with loud growls and barks.
What is a whiny dog trying to tell us?
The dog could be stressed or letting us know it's in pain.
When meeting a stranger or new canine pal, a dog might whine
if it feels threatened. An excited dog might wiggle and whine,
and a hard-to-please pup might simply be demanding attention.

CLEVER CANINES

Brainy dogs can perform tricks, sniff out bombs, track down criminals, and round up sheep. Let's discover what makes a hound so helpful.

Why are dogs so easy to train?
Canines are pack animals and look to a group leader for instructions. When dogs live with humans, they bond with their human owner and look to them for direction.

How does a dog's brain compare to ours?
Scientists believe that a dog's understanding is similar to that of a 2- to 5-year-old child. Dogs work out which dog bowl contains the most food, notice when we point to an object, identify familiar voices, and judge whether someone is a friend or an enemy.

What's unique about a dog's brain?

A big dog has a lemon-sized brain, with a similar structure to most other mammals' brains. However, a dog uses a much larger portion of its brain for examining smells. In fact, the smell section of a dog's brain, called the olfactory bulb, is proportionally about 40 times bigger than a human's!

That's not to be sniffed at! Is this why dogs are super-trackers?

The super-sized odor analyzer in a dog's brain, combined with its 300 million scent receptors, means that a dog has an awesome sense of smell. Scientists believe that clever canines could sniff out a teaspoon of sugar in two Olympic-sized swimming pools of water!

Does this make them the animal kingdom's champion super-smeller?

A Bloodhound's odor detection rate is hundreds of times better than a human's. However, you might want to sniff out a bear's sense of smell, which is thousands of times better than ours!

PUPPY POWER!

Which capable canines have been trained to take on valuable work? Let's hear it for these paw-esome pups!

What major jobs have dogs taken on?

Sled dogs have been used in the Arctic for over 9,000 years, where indigenous peoples invented and perfected dogsled travel. During the Alaskan Gold Rush in the late 1890's, camps were only accessible in winter by dogsled. They brought in vital supplies, mail, prospectors, trappers, and even doctors!

Did city-dwelling dogs haul things around, too?

In streets too narrow for horse-drawn carts, people used dog carts. Pups delivered bread, milk, and groceries, and they could be relied upon to guard the load, too!

That sounds exhausting! What other historical assignments were dogs given?

The turnspit was a standard piece of equipment in a large 16th-century kitchen. Dogs were trained to run on a wheel that turned meat on a spit next to the fire, to make sure that the meat roasted evenly. Let's hope the dogs got the leftover bones at the end of the meal!

Cats are famous for their rat- and mouse-catching skills. Were any canines entrusted with this job?

In the mid-19th century, Billy the Terrier and his owner Jack Black appointed themselves official rat catchers to Queen Victoria. Billy caught thousands of rats hidden under floorboards and down in the sewers, and in doing so made his rat-bitten master quite famous! Chinese Crested Dogs were taken on board ships to hunt rats below deck. They would be traded among sailors traveling from port to port, so this breed soon popped up around the world!

What's the most unusual job a dog has had?

In Peru, archaeologists have discovered mummies buried in ancient tombs, filled with jewelry, masks, headdresses, and ornaments made from gold and semi-precious stones. One mummified ruler, the Lord of Sipan, was laid to rest alongside his favorite pet pooch. According to local folklore, the dog's job may have been to guide his master to the afterworld!

Let's get up to speed with the productive pups of today.
What jobs do dogs take on?
A sniffer dog is trained to detect explosives, illegal goods, missing persons, and lawbreakers. Bio detection dogs can be used to detect human diseases, and help doctors catch illnesses early.

What other ways can dogs help with medical problems?
Guide dogs help blind or visually impaired people navigate, leading them around obstacles they can't see. A dog needs 3 to 6 months of training to become a certified guide dog.

Are there dogs that help with hearing, too?

A **hearing dog** can alert a deaf person to doorbells, telephone calls, timers, and smoke alarms.

Can dogs help people with other disabilities?

Assistance dogs can provide a helping paw with daily tasks such as unloading the washing machine, shopping, and opening and closing doors. They can also help people with post-traumatic stress disorder, autistic people, and others who could use a supportive paw handle stressful situations.

Do dogs have an important role in hospitals?

Therapy dogs comfort patients suffering from both mental and physical illness in hospitals. Studies have found that dogs recognize when someone needs care and attention, and nervous children waiting to see a doctor feel calmer when a dog is around. A **medical detection dog** can identify an owner's epileptic seizure up to 50 minutes before it happens, or spot when a diabetic's sugar levels are too low.

MAN'S BEST FRIEND

When did dogs first become pets? Let's high-tail it back to the very beginning and find out!

How do we know when dogs were domesticated?

Experts think that dogs were one of the earliest pets. Dog bones have been found beside human skeletons in graves that are thousands of years old.

How long have dogs existed?

The dates are a little hazy, but some of the oldest fossilized dog remains are around 33,000 years old. What scientists do agree on is that our house-trained pups can be traced back 15,000 to 40,000 years to just one source . . . wolves!

How did fearsome and aggressive wolves become cute and cuddly pooches? Here's the theory. Let's say a pack of wolves circled a camp of early human hunters to sniff out some leftovers. A wolf that was tamer and less threatening would be tolerated by the humans, and so that wolf would pick up more scraps. Humans would develop a relationship with the gentler wolves, and over time these creatures would go through changes to become domesticated dogs. The process of creatures changing over time is called **evolution**.

18

When early humans befriended the more affectionate wolves, the trainable puppies were kept by humans, grew up, and had puppies of their own. Eventually, humans needed dogs with particular talents to help with different jobs. Farmers needed dogs to protect their livestock from predators, and hunters needed dogs with a great sense of smell, speed, and endurance. When humans began to live in communities, they looked for small, easy-going dogs to keep at home. The different dogs the humans chose for different tasks had puppies with each other, and became more and more different over time and many generations. When humans choose which dogs have puppies together because they want the puppies to have specific attributes, it's called **breeding**.

What sort of dogs were bred first?

Early dogs were probably bred for hunting. A set of 11,500-year-old canine bones found in Jordan suggest that dogs lived and hunted alongside humans to catch small, speedy prey such as hares and foxes.

Is there any other evidence of an ancient dog breeding program?

Let's head to the freezing Zhokhov Island in the East Siberian Sea. Try and find it on a map! Researchers have analyzed 9,000-year-old canine bones and believe that ancient Arctic dwellers bred smaller dogs to pull sleds, and larger mutts to hunt polar bears.

How many dog breeds do we have today?

It depends who you ask! At the time of writing, the **World Canine Organization** (better known as **Fédération Cynologique Internationale**) says there are 344 breeds of dog. **The American Kennel Club** lists 202 different breeds.

Which are the most ancient dog breeds still around today?

Take a look!

CHOW-CHOW

Where did it come from? China
When did it first appear? Around 200 BCE
Is there a fun fact about this breed?
In China, these dogs are known as Songshi-Quan, which translates to "puffy-lion dog"!

CHINESE SHAR PEI

Where did it come from? China
When did it first appear? Around 200 BCE
What was this dog bred for?
To hunt, and protect its owner's home and livestock.

SALUKI

Where did it come from? The Middle East
When did it first appear? As early as 7000 BCE
What are this dog's strengths?
This ancient hunting dog was bred for its power, endurance, and speed, and it can clock up to 42.8 mph (68.8 km/h) when running.

SAMOYED

Where did it come from? Siberia
When did it first appear? As early as 1000 BCE
Do these dogs make good pets?
Yes! They are intelligent, playful, and loyal.

ALASKAN MALAMUTE

Where did it come from? Alaska
When did it first appear? As early as 1000 BCE
What was this breed used for?
This dog is incredibly strong, so was used to pull loaded sleds.

AFGHAN HOUND

Where did it come from? The Middle East, or Asia
When did it first appear? Around 6000 BCE
How did this breed make it to Afghanistan?
Ancient rock carvings indicate that this dog traveled into the country when Alexander the Great invaded Afghanistan in 330 BCE.

BASENJI

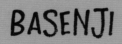

Where did it come from? Central Africa
When did it first appear? Around 6000 BCE or earlier
What is unusual about this breed? They are known as the "barkless" dog. Instead they whine, scream, and yodel!

AKITA INU

Where did it come from? Japan
When does it date from? Possibly 8000 BCE
Is there a fun fact about this breed?
They are named after a mountainous, snowy region in Japan. As they're built for their mountainous namesake, they have a thick double coat to keep out the cold and webbed paws to help them walk on snow.

MUTT MYTHS AND MYSTERIES

It's time to uncover the legends that have been linked to our four-legged-friends! Enjoy these stories and sagas.

Why did dogs choose to live with humans?

Let's take a look at this traditional story from the Native American Menominee tribe. A dog lived with the wolves, and they told him to steal fire from a man's wigwam. This was a dangerous job for the dog, as the humans, who feared wolves, might attack him. As he entered the wigwam, he noticed that the man was away, with just the women and children at home. He looked at everyone with friendly eyes, then crept over to the fire and laid down. The man that lived in the wigwam had dreamt that one day he would receive a gift from the wolves, and when he returned, he told the dog that they would forever be brothers. The man and the dog became hunting companions and friends.

Why does the Shih Tzu have a white spot on its head?

The legend goes that the Buddha was on a journey with his small dog when a gang attacked him. The pup transformed into a ferocious lion and chased the robbers away. The thankful Buddha kissed the Shih Tzu on its forehead, giving it the distinctive white mark.

Pugs are an honored breed in China. Why is this?

These dogs were the favorites of ancient Chinese rulers. In fact, the Emperor Ling of Han gave a favorite Pug a prestigious literary award. The Chinese believed that the distinctive wrinkles on a Pug's face formed a pattern similar to the Chinese character for "prince."

Why do Pembroke Welsh Corgis have a white strip on their backs?

The story goes that these pooches lived alongside elves and fairies. Their characteristic white markings show where fairies attached their saddles and harnesses before riding the Corgis into battle. Sounds like a perfectly reasonable explanation!

The lion-like Chow-Chow has a unique blue tongue. What's the story behind that?

According to the legend, this pup was allowed to lick up the tiny bits of blue sky that fell to Earth when the stars were put in place. I'll let you decide if that tale is true!

PUPS AROUND THE PLANET

Let's take a trip to meet the most popular pooches around the world.

There seem to be so many different dogs. How are the breeds categorized?
People group dog breeds in different ways! Here's one system:

SPORTING DOG
Why are these dogs called sporting dogs? These dogs were traditionally used for hunting and retrieving—or in other words, sports!
Example: Pointer

TOY DOG
Are these dogs really toys? No, but they're small and popular household pals, just like toys.
Example: Pomeranian

HERDING DOG
Why are these dogs called herding dogs? These highly-trainable dogs are skilled at moving livestock, or herding.
Example: Collie

HOUND DOG
What makes a hound a hound? These dogs are fast and have a great sense of smell, which made them handy in the past for tracking prey.
Example: Greyhound

TERRIER
What can these dogs do? These dogs were bred to catch rabbits and rats.
Example: American Pitbull Terrier

WORKING DOG
What makes a working dog a working dog? These breeds need plenty of exercise and can be used as guard and service dogs.
Example: Rottweiler

NON-SPORTING
"Non-sporting"? What does that mean? It means these dogs don't fit into any of the categories above, but they still make great companions!
Example: Poodle

JACK RUSSELL (Terrier)
Where are they from? England

What are these dogs like?
They have a strong will and lots of energy.

Do you have a fun fact about these dogs?
They can jump five times their own height!

SHIH TZU (Toy Dog)
Where are they from? Tibet

What does their name mean?
Little Lion
How long have Shih Tzus been around?
Over 1,000 years!

DACHSHUND, OR WIENER DOG (Hound Dog)
Where were they first bred? Germany

What were these dogs used for?
They were bred to hunt badgers.
What are some notable wiener dogs?
Pop artist Andy Warhol used to bring his Dachshund to interviews, and let the dog "answer" any difficult questions!

WEIMARANER (Sporting Dog)
Where are they from? They come from the Weimar region of Germany.
Do these dogs make good pets? This is a very energetic breed, so they need lots of exercise every day.

Are they trainable dogs?
Weimaraners are very smart, which makes training easier. It also means that they're good at unlocking gates and escaping!

YORKSHIRE TERRIER (Terrier)

Where are they from? England

What was this dog used for? These fierce, compact pooches were used by miners and weavers to hunt rats.

What's a famous face among terriers?
A Yorkshire Terrier called Smoky became one of the first therapy dogs when he toured hospitals after World War II to comfort wounded soldiers.

POODLE (Non-Sporting Dog)

Where are they from? People aren't sure whether the breed comes from the German Water Dog or the French Barbet.

Are there different types of poodle?
There are three varieties: standard, miniature, and toy. The Poodle comes in a wide assortment of colors, including white, black, brown, blue, gray, silver, café au lait, silver-beige, cream, apricot, and red!

BORDER COLLIE (Herding Dog)

Where were they first bred? U.K.

Is this breed easy to train?
These hard-working dogs learn words and commands and make champion sheep-herders. In fact, a Border Collie called Chaser learned to understand the names of more than 1,000 objects!

BOXER (Working Dog)

Where are they from? Germany

Do these dogs make good pets? These pups are known as the "Peter Pan" of dog breeds, as they take at least 3 years to grow up and act like adult dogs!

What else makes the Boxer unusual?
Boxers sometimes look like they're snoozing with their eyes open.

MINIATURE SCHNAUZER (Sporting Dog)
Where are they from? Germany

How do they behave?
They may be small, but these lively, playful, and feisty dogs are not afraid of a tussle when confronted by unfamiliar mutts.

What does their name mean?
Schnauzer is the German word for "beard."

GOLDEN RETRIEVER (Sporting Dog)
Where were these dogs first bred? Scotland
Why was this dog bred? This dog was used to retrieve ducks and other game birds during hunting parties.

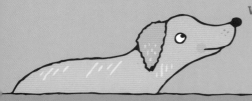

Why are Golden Retrievers such popular pets?
These dogs are calm, clever, and affectionate. They are easy to please, playful, and patient with children.

GERMAN SHEPHERD (Herding Dog)
Where are they from? Germany

What are this breed's best attributes? This dog is clever, hard-working, and easy to train. During World War I, these dogs brought first-aid to injured soldiers and delivered messages on the front line.

Which dog was the most famous German Shepherd?
Rin Tin Tin was rescued from a World War I battlefield, brought back to America, and became a celebrated movie star!

SIBERIAN HUSKY (Working Dog)

Where are they from? Siberia

What are their physical attributes?
These pups are born to run and make excellent sled dogs.

How do they cope with the cold?
They have a warm double coat, as well as almond-shaped eyes that allow them to keep out the snow when they squint.

LABRADOODLE (Sporting Dog)

Where was this dog first bred? Australia

When did this breed first appear?
1989. It's a cross between a Labrador Retriever and a Poodle.

Do they make good pets?
Like Labradors, they are great family dogs, and like poodles they are intelligent and protective.

ENGLISH SPRINGER SPANIEL (Sporting Dog)

Where are they from? England

How do these dogs behave?
They were originally bred as hunting dogs, so these athletic pups need plenty of exercise. Keep them on a leash, though, as they may go off hunting on their own!

Who were the most famous Springer Spaniels?
President George W. Bush had an English Springer Spaniel called Spot, and President George H.W. Bush had one named Millie!

FRENCH BULLDOG (Toy Dog)

Where does this breed come from?
They're a crossbreed between French ratter dogs and toy bulldogs imported into France from England.

What were these dogs used for? English lace-makers used these mini-mutts as lap-warmers to keep them cozy as they worked.

What sets these puppies apart? They can't swim, but they're chatty! They love to "talk" in gargles, squeaks, and yaps.

COCKAPOO

Where are they from? U.S.

What is a Cockapoo?
It's a cross between a Cocker Spaniel and a Poodle.
The breed dates back to the 1960s.

What are their best qualities?
When asked to choose one word to describe their dog, 70% of Cockapoo owners chose the word "friendly"!

CHIHUAHUA (Toy Dog)

Where are they from? Mexico

What is this dog's claim to fame? This pocket-sized pooch is the world's smallest breed, so it is ideal for people living in apartments or small houses.

Does this mean that these dogs are shy and nervous?
Far from it! In Colorado, a five-pound (2.3 kg) Chihuahua called Zoey bravely leapt in front of a venomous rattlesnake to protect her owner's one-year-old grandson. Despite being bitten, Zoey survived after receiving veterinary care.

BEAGLE (Hound)

Where does this breed come from? Not known, but Beagle-like dogs can be traced back 2,000 years to ancient Greece.

What is its best attribute? Its sense of smell. It's used in airports to detect forbidden food hidden in luggage.

Why do beagles have white tails?
They were bred that way! Originally, they were used to hunt rabbits, so they often had their heads down a burrow or against the ground. Distinctive, wagging tails made them a snap for their owners to find!

LABRADOR RETRIEVER (Sporting Dog)

Where does this breed come from?
Newfoundland

What were these dogs bred for?
With their waterproof coats and webbed toes, this breed was used by fishermen to catch escaped fish, bring in nets, and pull along boats by a rope.

What are they used for today?
Around 70% of all U.S. guide dogs are Labradors. They are the perfect size, versatile, and eager to please.

MIXED-BREED MUTTS

What is a mutt? It's a dog that doesn't belong to one of the officially recognized breeds, and is also known as a mongrel.

What's so great about a mutt? They can be healthier and happier, as they may not suffer from the illnesses, genetic conditions, or behavior issues that can be found in certain breeds.

HUGE HOUNDS AND MINIATURE MONGRELS

Are you ready for the 100 Questions Canine Contest? Prepare for some record-breaking pups!

We know that Chihuahuas are the smallest dog breed. How tiny do these mini-mutts get?

Let's hear it for Milly, who stood about 3.8 inches (9.65 cm) tall. That's smaller than a smart phone! When she was born, this Chihuahua could fit in a teaspoon.

Let's go to the other end of the scale. Who's the world's tallest dog?

That title belongs to a gigantic Great Dane called Zeus. He measured a record-breaking 3.8 feet (1.12 m) tall. When he stood on his back legs, Zeus hit the 7.5-foot (2.26 m) mark. That's taller than a stack of seven cereal boxes!

Which fur-midable four-legged friend wins the heavy-weight award?
A St. Bernard named Benedictine weighed in at 367 lbs (166.5 kg). That's as big as a black bear! (Remember: It's important to give pets a healthy diet to keep them in good shape.)

Now for the world's longest dog.
Which pup stretched out and grabbed this title?
Zorba, an Old English Mastiff from London, measured an extraordinary 8.25 feet (2.5 m) from nose to tail. By comparison, a male lion is just a little over 6 feet (1.8 m) long. Or just imagine an adult man lying down!

Let's hear it for the dog with the longest ears.
Which paw-esome pooch wins that prize?
Tigger, a Bloodhound, holds that record. His right ear measured 13.75 inches
(34.9 cm) while his lengthy left ear measured 13.5 inches (34.2 cm).
That's almost as long as four Milly the Chihuahuas!

Now for the dog with the world's longest tongue.
Which record-breaking pup has got it licked?
Step up . . . Brandy the Boxer! His tongue measured a mind-boggling
17 inches (43 cm). Imagine three and a half cans of soda end to end!

It's time for the Waggiest World Record. Who is the dog with the longest tail? Here comes Keon, an Irish Wolfhound from Belgium. His tremendous tail measures 30.2 inches (76.8 cm), or longer than 4 bananas!

Which attention-seeking dog has got the loudest woof? A noisy Golden Retriever named Charlie barked at an ear-popping 113.1 decibels in 2012. That's louder than a chainsaw!

PRIZE-WINNING PUPS!

It's time to take a look at the high-achieving hounds who go above and beyond.

Which breed of dog is the fastest?
The Greyhound can run at a super-speedy 43 mph (70 km/h). That's on four legs, though. Even more impressive is Konjo, a Californian mixed-breed pup who scurried along a 16-foot (5 m) course on just her two front legs in a record-smashing time of 2.39 seconds.

Now for the high jump! Which powerful pooch has leapt into the record books?
A Greyhound called Feather set the high-jumping record by leaping a remarkable 6'3" (1.92 m). That's almost as high as a door!

Let's stay in the Leaping League! What is the record for the longest jump?
Do you think a dog could jump farther than the length of a bus?
Well, a Whippet named Sounders did! He took part in a dock jumping
contest and caused an enormous splash with his prize-winning
leap of 36'2" (11.02 m).

Which disciplined dog wins the Top Tricks trophy?
A round of applause for Hero! This Border Collie performed a record-breaking
49 tricks in just a minute. His selection of skills included dancing,
rolling over, and catching a Frisbee!

Have any multi-talented mutts claimed more than one top title?
Let's say hello to Norman, who has hit the record books twice! In 2013,
he completed a 98-foot (30 m) course on a scooter in just 20.77 seconds. Just
under a year later, this record-breaker traveled the same distance on a bicycle
in a stunning 55.41 seconds. That's wheel-y great!

Which dogs are champion dog-paddlers?
First up is a champion swimmer called Umbra, a Labrador/Greyhound cross.
She swam 3 miles (4.8 km) in a record time of 85 minutes, and was the only
recorded dog to have swum the Bosphorus Sea from Asia to Europe.

Abbie-girl is a daredevil dog who not only skydives, but is also a super-surfer!
She gained recognition by surfing a 351'8" (107.2 m) long wave—the longest
surfed by a dog on record!

Which prize-winning paw-ticipants might be worth signing on to a sports team?

Do you play soccer? Then take a look at Purin the Beagle as a possible goalkeeper. This coordinated canine took just one minute to catch 14 balls with his paws. Alternatively, you could use Finley as a ball boy. This good-natured Golden Retriever can fit six tennis balls in his mouth. He is now sitting patiently as he waits for his record to be recognized.

Which heroic hound has hit dizzying heights in her record attempt?

In 2018, a stray dog called Mera tagged along with a climbing group in the Himalayas and shared the leader's tent and food. Mera successfully reached the top of Baruntse's peak, just south of Mount Everest. That's a height of 23,389 feet (7,129 m), or nearly 19 Empire State Buildings tall!

TOP TAIL-WAGGERS

Let's take a trip to the Hound Hall of Fame and check out some well-known woofers!

Which distinguished dogs should we applaud for their heroic actions?
There's a long list, but let's start with Barry the St. Bernard. He worked as a 19th century mountain rescue dog in Switzerland, and would sniff out climbers trapped by an avalanche. Legend has it that his efforts saved over 40 lives, including a freezing boy whom he warmed up by licking him, before carrying him to safety.

Are there any other dogs that are famous for their daring deeds?
In 1828, a ship traveling from Ireland to Quebec hit a rock off Newfoundland. The shipwrecked survivors managed to cling to rocks, but because of the wind, rain, and heavy waves, a rescue party led by fisherman George Harvey could only get within 100 feet (30 m) of the island. George's dog, a Newfoundland called Hairy Man, dove into the water carrying a rope to create a lifeline. The ship's passengers and crew were able to follow the rope to the rescue boat, and 152 people survived!

What makes a Newfoundland such a first-rate rescue dog?

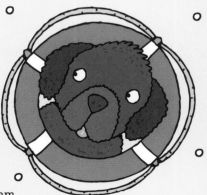

- They are large and muscular, so they're capable of pulling a human in water.

- They have webbed feet, which makes them excellent swimmers.

- Their double coat is waterproof and protects them from the cold.

  In fact, this breed is part of the sea rescue team in Italy. They are trained to jump out of helicopters, and with their help, the team saves about 3,000 stranded swimmers each year.

**Such courage! Which determined dog played a
vital role in saving a whole town?**

Let's head back to 1925. A deadly epidemic broke out in the remote Alaskan town
of Nome, threatening the population of around 10,000 people. The good news was
there was a cure. The bad news was that this cure was 674 miles (1,085 km) away,
and the extreme winter weather meant that rail or air travel was impossible.
The only option was to get the medicine by sled dog teams. The hero of the
Great Race of Mercy was a 12-year-old Siberian Husky called Togo. With his
musher Leonhard Seppala, Togo led his dog team over 264 miles (425 km)
to help deliver the vital vaccine. In 2001, this extraordinary dog was
honored with a statue in New York's Seward Park.

Have any military mutts shown bravery on the battlefield?

Stubby was the official mascot of the 102nd Infantry Regiment (U.S.), and took part
in 17 battles in World War I. He alerted his unit to incoming shells, sniffed out gas
before the human soldiers could, located and comforted wounded soldiers, and
even captured an enemy spy. His commander was so impressed that he nominated
Stubby for promotion to the rank of sergeant!

Which pampered pooches have been spoiled rotten by kings and queens?
Let's begin by traveling back 4,000 years to ancient Egypt. We know of a pharaoh's guard dog called Abuwtiyuw. Upon his death, this magnificent mutt was honored with an elaborate ceremony; wrapped in fine, perfumed linen; and finally buried in an ornamental stone tomb.

He must have been a first-rate guard dog! Which other rulers had a fondness for our four-legged friends?
Henry III of France had hundreds of dogs who were looked after by servants, governesses, and a personal baker who made them fresh white loaves of bread each day. The king would often walk around Paris with a basket of pups hanging from his neck!

Which monarchs gave their dogs top priority?

After her five-hour coronation ceremony on June 28, 1838,
Queen Victoria had just one thing on her mind: she rushed back to
Buckingham Palace to give her dog Dash his nightly bath! Her son,
King Edward VII, was no different. He had a white Fox Terrier who wore
a tag on his collar which read, "I am Caesar. I belong to The King." When
his owner died in 1910, Caesar was heartbroken, and would search the
palace looking for the king. The faithful dog led his funeral march.

These pups lived a life of luxury.
Which ruler's generosity was a little over the top?

If you were a dog, you might want to be the Maharaja of Junagadh's pet. This
Indian ruler owned 800 pooches, each with its own room, servant, and telephone.
As a treat, he would dress the dogs in evening suits, then take them for an evening
drive in rickshaws. He spent a fortune on a three-day wedding ceremony between
his favorite pup, Roshanara, and a royal retriever called Bobby.

Have any of our four-legged friends become film stars?

A rough collie called Lassie is one of the world's most famous fictional pups. There have been over 10 *Lassie* films, as well as Lassie radio shows, TV programs, video games, and books. She even has her own star on the Hollywood Walk of Fame!

Which legendary dog had a real-life "rags to riches" story?

Terry was a Cairn Terrier who had been abandoned as a puppy. Luckily for her, she was rescued by a Hollywood dog trainer called Carl Spitz, who used silent hand signals to direct performing pups. Terry went on to star as Toto in *The Wizard of Oz*, one of the most memorable movie mutts!

We know that some dogs are more prized (and therefore expensive!) than others. How much can that doggy in the window cost?

Megan is a well-trained super-sheepdog who was sold to an Oklahoma farmer for a record-breaking $23,549 (£18,900). That's loose change compared to the sky-high $1.95 million (£1.59 million) that was handed over for a Tibetan Mastiff puppy. These dogs make loyal and protective pets, and this ancient breed is a valuable status symbol in China.

Are any dogs wealthy in their own right?

A German Shepherd called Gunther III tops the canine rich list. He inherited an eye-watering $65 million (£53 million) from his owner in 1992. With some help from his human investment team, this sum turned into a $375 million (£306 million) fortune, which was passed on to his heir, Gunther IV.

IT'S A DOG'S LIFE

There are around 90 million pet pooches in the USA alone! Interested in your own furry friend? Here's what you need to know.

Would a dog take up much of my time?

First, dogs live for an average of 13 years, so make sure that you're really dedicated to the idea of a four-legged friend. A new dog will have a big impact on your life too. You'll need to commit some time each day for training, playtime, and exercise, as well as feeding and grooming your dog.

What do I need to think about before choosing a dog?

- Can a dog fit in with your family? Are you too busy to train, exercise, feed, and care for a furry friend? Also: Many breeds of dog don't get along with young children. Do you have any younger brothers or sisters?

- Do you want a puppy or a dog? Puppies in particular need a lot of attention, help with toilet training, and a regular routine.

- Do you have the outside space that some breeds might need? If you live in a small apartment without a backyard, then a large, energetic dog might not be a great choice.

- Are you ready to "pooch-proof" your home? You might discover puppy poop on a rug, or bite marks on your favorite sneakers. Training is the answer to these little hiccups!

- Some people are allergic to dogs. They may start to cough, sneeze, get itchy eyes, or develop rashes. Is anyone in your family allergic?

What equipment would I need to buy?

Looking after a dog can be expensive. Here's a list of essentials:

- FOOD, AND TREATS FOR TRAINING
- WATER BOWLS
- LEASH AND COLLAR
- TOYS
- BED AND BEDDING
- POO BAGS
- DOG CRATE
- BRUSH AND DOG SHAMPOO

You'll also need to consider pet insurance, veterinary bills, grooming services, training classes, and, if you go on vacation, a pet sitting service or boarding kennel.

What food do pups enjoy?

Ask your vet, as it's all down to the individual dog. It's important that every pooch receive a healthy and balanced diet tailored to the dog's age and any medical issues it might have. The amount of food your dog needs will depend on its size, age, breed, and how much exercise it gets. Don't underfeed or overfeed your pup, and keep it well hydrated at all times.

Okay! I'm in! How do I find the right dog?

You could start with a dog shelter or rescue center. Their dedicated staff will match you and your lifestyle with the right four–legged friend. They will have hounds of all shapes and sizes! A vet will check the dog from nose to tail, and give it all the necessary treatments and vaccinations. They'll provide you with background information about your new dog, and their help and advice will give you confidence as you get to know your new pet at home.

I might want a purebred dog. How should I go about choosing the best breed?
You might not want to hear this, but **do your homework!** Some breeds like
a quiet space of their own, and others like a rowdy family atmosphere.
There are breeds that love to please, and others that are not quite so obedient.
Shelters house some purebred dogs, or you could contact organizations
who keep lists of trustworthy breeders.

Okay . . . I've done my research and selected the best dog for my family. What should I look for when I'm trying to choose my four-legged friend?

● If it's a puppy you're after, see how the pups interact with each other. You're looking for a confident puppy that is neither bossy nor meek.

● A good tip is to take a toy and a handful of soft chicken treats when you go to meet a potential pooch. A dog should take the treats gently, and want to play with the toy. If the dog isn't interested in the treat, it may be afraid or ill.

● If you pick up a puppy, does it settle down fairly quickly? See how comfortable the dog is when you lift, carry, or handle it. Take a look at the dog's teeth (they should look sharp!), check the ears and eyes for injuries or bugs, lift the paws, and give the pooch a hug. Some dogs are cautious around strangers, so ask for help if you're a little unsure.

● Does the dog have a healthy, shiny coat? Does it look like it's at a healthy weight? A puppy shouldn't be too plump or too skinny.

● Ask if you can take the pup for a walk. How does the dog behave on a leash? Is the dog comfortable around children, adults, and other animals?

● Some rescued dogs have behavioral and physical challenges, which can be overcome in their new home with your family's love and support.

HOUSE AND HOUND

You've chosen your four-legged friend! Here are some tips to make your dog feel at home!

What can I do before my new pup comes home?
Make sure your home and garden are secure so your inquisitive pup can't escape! Select a quiet place where your dog is going to sleep, and have a bed, bowl of water, toy, and a blanket ready.

What does the whole family need to do?
Make sure that everyone is consistent about sticking to the rules. A dog gets confused if one person allows it to jump onto the couch, then another person tells it off for doing so.

When my dog comes home, what should the first thing I do be?
It's normal for a new dog to feel anxious or scared in its new home, so your first step is to make it feel comfortable! Keep calm, and gently stroke your pet. It will take a little while for trust to grow, so let the dog take its time to build a bond with you. Give it space to explore, and try not to play too roughly at first.

How do I train my dog?
Keep it simple! Start with the main commands of sit, stay, and down, then compliment or reward your dog when it does what you asked.

You've learned so much doggy data and uncovered some super scoops.
I think it's time for a walk!

CHECK OUT ALL OF THE FANTASTIC FACTS IN THIS SENSATIONAL SERIES!

100 Questions about the
Amazon Rainforest

100 Questions about Bugs

100 Questions about Cats

100 Questions about Colonial America

100 Questions about Dinosaurs

100 Questions about Dogs

100 Questions about Extreme Weather

100 Questions about the Human Body

100 Questions about Oceans

100 Questions about Outer Space

100 Questions about Pirates

100 Questions about Rocks & Minerals

100 Questions about Sharks

100 Questions about Spies